Draw your portrait in the frame

THIS BOOK BELONGS TO:

_____

_____

 CHICAGO REVIEW PRESS

Tag and Share your Creations:

#ColorfulWyomingJournal

Written **and** illustrated in Colorado.

ALL MY LIFE THROUGH,
THE NEW SIGHTS OF NATURE
MADE ME REJOICE LIKE A CHILD.

—MARIE CURIE

Colorful Wyoming

Welcome to the Wild West with dramatic vistas, epic mountain ranges, parks,
monuments, winding rivers, hot springs, and geysers. These boundless landscapes
are home to a distinct variety of animals and plant life. In 1872, Yellowstone
National Park became the nation's first National Park.

THE VIEW OF EARTH
IS SPECTACULAR.

—SALLY RIDE

Grizzly Bears in Yellowstone National Park

Grizzly Bears can be difficult to differentiate from Black Bears, as they also range in color from black to blonde. Grizzlies have unique features; a pronounced shoulder hump, smaller ears, a more concave face, and much larger claws. In Wyoming they are a an integral part of the Greater Yellowstone Ecosystem.

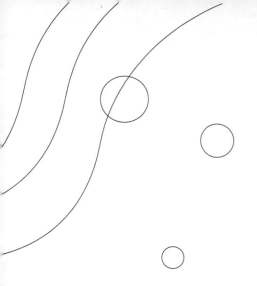

STUDY NATURE,
LOVE NATURE,
STAY CLOSE TO NATURE.
IT WILL NEVER FAIL YOU.

—FRANK LLOYD WRIGHT

Cutthroat Trout

Wyoming's State fish, and native species to western North America, is known
for dark spots and bright orange marks on the sides of the throat.
Cutthroat return to their native stream to spawn.

LOOK DEEP INTO NATURE
AND THEN YOU WILL UNDERSTAND
EVERYTHING BETTER.

—ALBERT EINSTEIN

Red Fox overlooking Green River Lake

Resourceful and cunning, the Red Fox is highly adaptable to wide varieties of
habitat and diet. They can vary in color, but always have a white-tipped tail.

IT IS ONLY IN THE CONDITION OF HUMILITY
AND REVERENCE BEFORE THE WORLD
THAT OUR SPECIES WILL BE ABLE TO REMAIN IN IT.

— WENDELL BERRY

Grey Wolf

Reintroduced to Yellowstone National Park in 1995, wolves are a key component
to a healty ecosystem. They control populations of their prey providing a rippling
effect to the health of the entire environ. They live and hunt in packs of 7-8,
and communicate using a large repitoir of barks, whines, and growls.

I HAVE NEVER SEEN A WILDFLOWER
IN ALL ITS BEAUTY BE ASHAMED
OF WHERE IT GROWS
—MICHAEL XAVIER

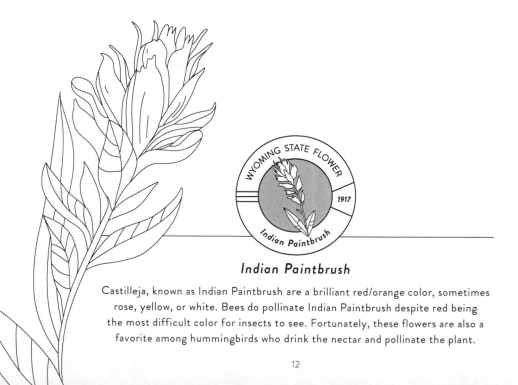

Indian Paintbrush

Castilleja, known as Indian Paintbrush are a brilliant red/orange color, sometimes rose, yellow, or white. Bees do pollinate Indian Paintbrush despite red being the most difficult color for insects to see. Fortunately, these flowers are also a favorite among hummingbirds who drink the nectar and pollinate the plant.

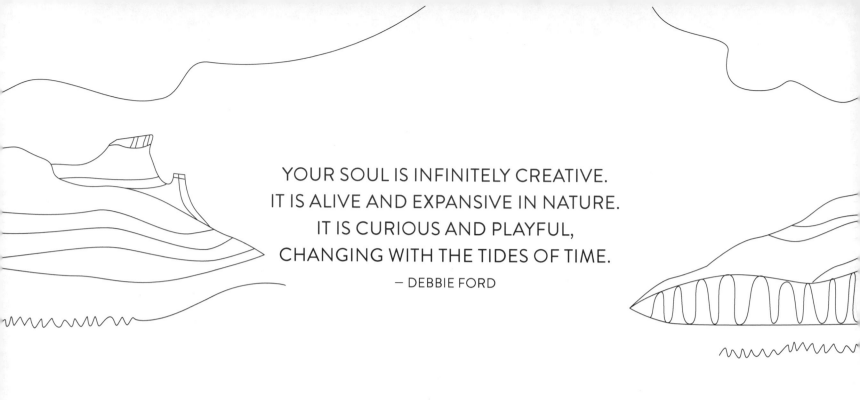

YOUR SOUL IS INFINITELY CREATIVE.
IT IS ALIVE AND EXPANSIVE IN NATURE.
IT IS CURIOUS AND PLAYFUL,
CHANGING WITH THE TIDES OF TIME.

– DEBBIE FORD

Wild Horses

Wild horses are the free-spirited symbol of the "Wild West". Wyoming is home
to the second largest population of wild horses in the nation. Sixteen herds roam
five million acres of unfenced-land mainly located in the southwestern portion
of the state.

TODAY IS YOUR DAY!
YOUR MOUNTAIN IS WAITING.
SO... GET ON YOUR WAY!

−DR. SEUSS

Elk in the Wind River Range

Elk are also called "Wapiti", a Native American word that means
"light-colored deer." Females are called 'cows' and males 'bulls'.
The bull's antlers can grow up to an inch a day.

WE STAND SOMEWHERE BETWEEN
THE MOUNTAIN AND THE ANT.

— NATIVE AMERICAN (ONONDAGA) PROVERB

Beavers

These industrious creatures are gentle, intelligent, and crafty beings who even like
to play practical jokes. They are integral in a healthy environment; pruning the
forest and creating watery habitats for a variety of mammals, birds and reptiles.

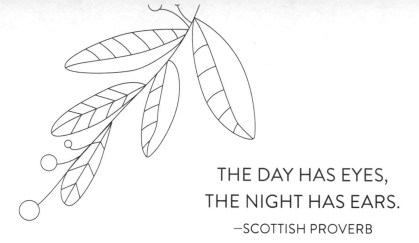

THE DAY HAS EYES,
THE NIGHT HAS EARS.

—SCOTTISH PROVERB

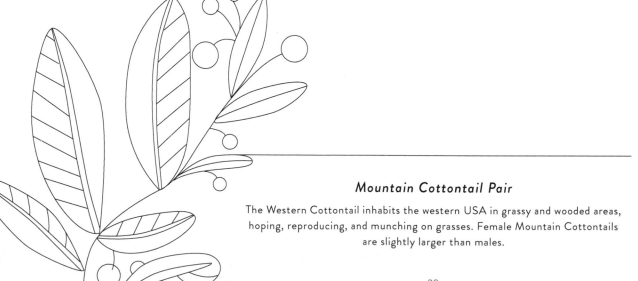

Mountain Cottontail Pair

The Western Cottontail inhabits the western USA in grassy and wooded areas,
hoping, reproducing, and munching on grasses. Female Mountain Cottontails
are slightly larger than males.

THERE IS NO BETTER DESIGNER THAN NATURE.

—ALEXANDER MCQUEEN

Sage-Grouse in Sagebrush

A symbol of the western sagebrush plains, the Sage-Grouse is a large, chubby bird with a small head. When males are "displaying" to attract a mate, they fan out their tail feathers and expand two yellow air sacks making gurgling and popping sounds. Recent development has decressed habitat and populations.

NATURE ALWAYS WEARS
THE COLORS OF THE SPIRIT.

—RALPH WALDO EMERSON

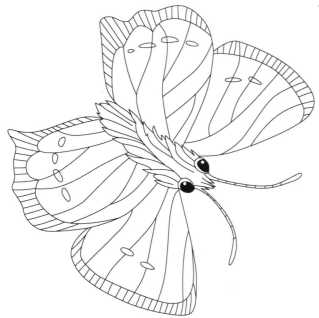

Sheridan's Green Hairstreak Butterfly resting on Goldenrod

This striking butterfly was originally discovered in Sheridan, Wyoming. A
beautiful green insect, it's arrival signals the beginning of spring in Wyoming's
mountains and foothills.

NATURE GIVES TO EVERY TIME AND SEASON
SOME BEAUTIES OF ITS OWN .

—CHARLES DICKENS

Bison Family in the Yellowstone National Park

The largest mammal in North America, the Bison was almost hunted to extinction by European settlers. Recent efforts and restrictions have restored their numbers. Bison calves are born a red/orange color. That turns chocolate brown like their parents, as they age.

ADOPT THE PACE OF NATURE:
HER SECRET IS PATIENCE.

—RALPH WALDO EMERSON

White-Tailed Deer

The smallest member of the North American deer family, the
White-Tailed deer is fast and agile. They can run up to 30 mph, jump
up to 10 feet high, and bound as far as 30 feet to outmanuver predators.

THE EARTH HAS MUSIC
FOR THOSE WHO LISTEN.
—WILLIAM SHAKESPEARE

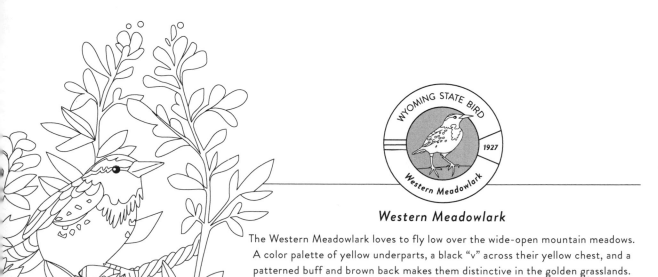

WYOMING STATE BIRD

1927

Western Meadowlark

Western Meadowlark

The Western Meadowlark loves to fly low over the wide-open mountain meadows. A color palette of yellow underparts, a black "v" across their yellow chest, and a patterned buff and brown back makes them distinctive in the golden grasslands.

TO SIT IN THE SHADE ON A FINE DAY,
AND LOOK UPON VERDURE,
IS THE MOST PERFECT REFRESHMENT.

—JANE AUSTEN, *Mansfield Park*

Pika in the Grand Tetons

Pikas live at elevations above 11,000ft. Their brown, peppery colored fur lets them blend into rocky terrain where they create connected dens. They are susceptible to global warming, moving higher in search of cool temperatures.

NOT JUST BEAUTIFUL,
THOUGH--THE STARS ARE LIKE THE TREES IN THE FOREST,
ALIVE AND BREATHING. AND THEY'RE WATCHING ME.

—HARUKI MURAKAMI, *Kafka on the Shore*

Great-Horned Owl Pair

Common to North America, these owls don't actually have horns at all, but
feathery tufts called plumicorns. Nighttime predators, these owls have piercing
yellow eyes and deep, soft hoots.

OF ALL THE PATHS YOU TAKE IN LIFE,
MAKE SURE A FEW OF THEM ARE DIRT.

—JOHN MUIR

Bighorn Sheep

Both Rams (males) and Ewes (females) don curly horns. Males have larger horns used as weapons for protection and dominance. Excellent vision and split hooves prepare them for rough Rocky Mountain terrain.

THERE IS NO BETTER
DESIGNER THAN NATURE.
—ALEXANDER MCQUEEN

Horned Lizard

Horned Lizards range in color from yellow, brown, and reddish brown camouflaging to their surrounding. They snap up ants and other insects. They protect themselves by puffing up their bodies to twice the size, and confuse predators by shooting blood from their eyes that is poisonous to some.

HEAVEN IS UNDER OUR FEET
AS WELL AS OVER OUR HEADS.
—HENRY DAVID THOREAU, *Walden*

Moose

Moose are the largest member of the deer family. They are a velvety chocolate
brown color. Their long legs help them traverse snowy meadow, swim and they
can even run at speeds up to 35mph

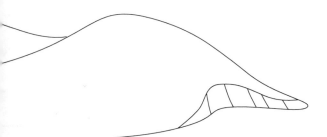

NATURE IS NOT
A PLACE TO VISIT.
IT IS HOME.
—GARY SNYDER

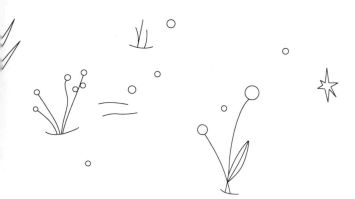

Coyotes

Native Americans have revered the coyote as a cunning creature. They have
cleverly adapted to change in the American landscape. Thriving in urban to
remote areas where they will eat almost anything.

I WONDER IF THE SNOW
LOVES THE TREES AND FIELDS,
THAT IT KISSES THEM SO GENTLY?
AND THEN IT COVERS THEM UP SNUG,
YOU KNOW, WITH A WHITE QUILT;
AND PERHAPS IT SAYS 'GO TO SLEEP, DARLINGS,
TILL THE SUMMER COMES AGAIN.'

—LEWIS CARROLL, *Alice's Adventures in Wonderland & Through the Looking-Glass*

Canada Lynx

The Lynx's long legs and distinctive large feet provide great mobility in
Colorado's snowy forests. These solitary creatures are protected under the
Endangered species act as threatened species.

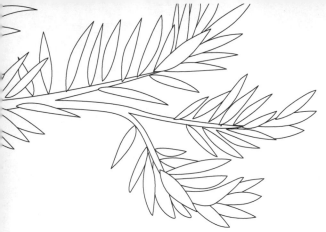

LIFE ITSELF IS THE MOST WONDERFUL FAIRYTALE.

—HANS CHRISTIAN ANDERSON

Porcupine

A porcupine can have up to 30,000 quills covering all of its body except the stomach. These quills are only used as self defense. Mostly solitary animals, porcupines are also excellent tree-climbers and swimmers.

NATURE IS NEW EVERY MORNING.

—PROVERB

Mountain Goats at Overlook

These high altitude mammals are covered in a white woolly coat. They live in alpine and sub-alpine regions often over 13,000ft in the summer. Males are called "billies", females "nannies", and their young are called "kids".

NATURE IS PLEASED WITH SIMPLICITY.
AND NATURE IS NO DUMMY.
—ISAAC NEWTON

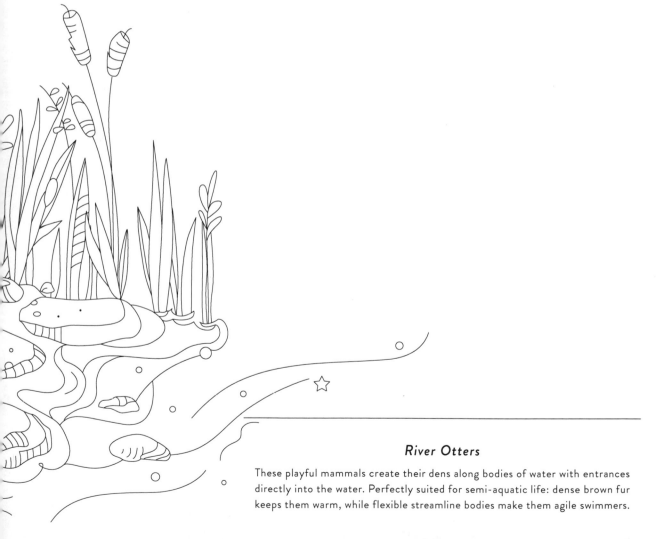

River Otters

These playful mammals create their dens along bodies of water with entrances directly into the water. Perfectly suited for semi-aquatic life: dense brown fur keeps them warm, while flexible streamline bodies make them agile swimmers.

HAPPINESS FLUTTERS IN THE AIR
WHILST WE REST AMONG
THE BREATHS OF NATURE.

—KELLY SHEAFFER

Pronghorn Antelope at Devil's Tower

Pronghorns are some of the fastest animals in North America,
reaching speeds of up to 53mph. They are a reddish brown color
with white bellies and white bands across their necks.

SPRING IS NATURE'S WAY OF SAYING,
'LET'S PARTY!'.
—ROBIN WILLIAMS

Broad-tailed Hummingbird in Agastache Flowers

These buzzing little jewels can be found in mountain meadows and forests darting
between blossoms. They eat mostly insects and nectar, preferring red tubular
flowers like the Agastache flowers.

EVERY SUNSET
BRINGS THE PROMISE
OF A NEW DAWN.

—RALPH WALDO EMERSON

Black Bear Sow and Cub

Black, brown, and even cinnamon in color, these intelligent creatures have a sense of smell 7 times more powerful than a bloodhound. They can smell food up to 20 miles away. In late fall they eat 20,000 calories a day to prepare for winter hibernation.

JUST LIVING IS NOT ENOUGH.
ONE MUST HAVE SUNSHINE, FREEDOM,
AND A LITTLE FLOWER.

— HANS CHRISTIAN ANDERSEN

Bumble Bees in Bee Balm flowers

A Bumble Bee's wings beat at 130 times or more per second. They are incredible
and essential pollinators. A threatened species, planting bumble bee gardens and
reducing pesticides can help save bumble bee's habitat and food sources.

...EARTH TEACH ME FREEDOM
AS THE EAGLE THAT SOARS IN THE SKY...

—UTE PRAYER

Golden Eagle in flight

This fast and nimble raptor is the ultimate predator of the skies. Magnificent in flight, it is a rich brown color with gold sheen at the back of the head and neck. Many Native American tribes revere the Golden Eagle for courage and strength.

COME FORTH INTO THE LIGHT OF THINGS,
LET NATURE BE YOUR TEACHER.

—WILLIAM WORDSWORTH

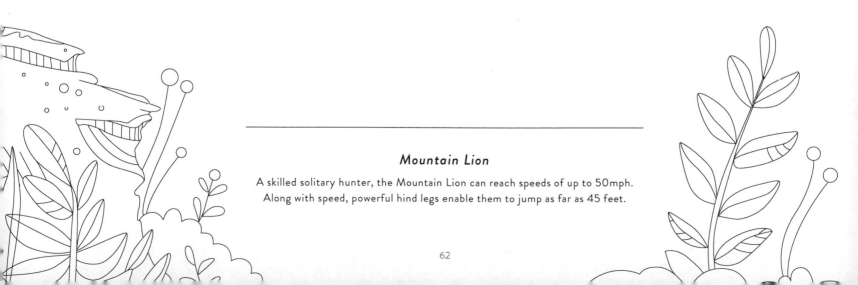

Mountain Lion

A skilled solitary hunter, the Mountain Lion can reach speeds of up to 50mph.
Along with speed, powerful hind legs enable them to jump as far as 45 feet.

AMANDA LENZ is a professional illustrator and nature lover. She paired her background in art and design with her love of the outdoors to develop the Colorful Wyoming Coloring Journal, featuring rich, nature-inspired illustrations meant to be unique artworks.